CANCER IN JANUARY

CAPRICORN IN SEPTEMBER

By Samuel I. Lora

PublishAmerica
Baltimore

ISBN: 1-60672-766-4
PUBLISHED BY PUBLISHAMERICA, LLLP
www.publishamerica.com
Baltimore

Printed in the United States of America

Appreciation

I want to thank the following people for making the past year more bearable.

TJ for giving me life again.
Trusting you again made wonders for my life.
Regardless of where our stars take us, you are engraved in my soul. I'm glad that we had a chance to share, I had a chance to need you again and you to protect me again.
I love you.

Tavis, for teaching me many-a-lessons, for pushing my buttons, for showing me who I want to be, who I want to be with, who cares for me, who I care for, and finally for being the biggest *pendejo*, most stubborn, yet most loving man someone can know.
You know I love you.

Krystifer thank you for the past, the present colliding, the future, for raw honesty and for unpredictable trips. I thank you for all you put in me.
I love you.

Mauricio for showing me what friends do for one another. Tan lindo tener un amigo como tu.
I love you.

David C. for international relations. The friendship we have goes beyond concerts, big cities, musical tastes, and breaking down personal barriers.
I learn from you. I learn from UZ.

Roberto for this opportunity; I don't know if you are aware, but you have a lot to do with this book being at all possible. Hell, for my first one to exist. I thank you for sharing with me the opportunity to finally close my mouth and open my heart.
Gracias Bebbo.

Shelly, Rosemary and Elizabeth for talking me through my pain. For entertaining me, for caring for me and loving me through all the mess that is our job. My daily routine would have sucked without you guys. And to Stephanie for a Thanksgiving miracle.

Heather for listening and sharing.

Kevin for distracting me.

Laura, Timmy, KC and Price for loving all of us and letting things be mild and less complicated.

Aaron for being so genuine and allowing all of us to see how much love you have within you.

Uncle Greg for making dad happy. You are his only brother and he loved you like it too.

Grandmother Dale for being such a support for grandpa, mom, Monica and I.
You're an unbelievable woman.

Aunt Tina and uncle Brian, you both drew a smile on that face. Thanks for cake, pizza and the most amazing memory of the period. I'm glad you guys were in his life and that you are both crazy enough to do everything you did to make him happy. You guys are beyond description. Thank you for all you did for us while we were going through this.
The three of us appreciate you to no limits.
Thank you truly.

Papa Roni for being you.
You talking to me opened the world and its possibilities. I will carry that moment forever.
Thank you for letting me see I'm made off your skin, veins, passionate living and winking, sparkling eyes.
I love you immensely.

Grammy for going through all that you did, for being an amazing grandmother, for your support, love and ability to become malleable after all the years.
You have shaped me and I hope to share more with you.
I love you tremendously.

Eduardito for coming over and over again to help us heal dad. Thank you for always believing and helping us who have lost faith along the way.
Thank you for holding dad with your healing hands and your willing mind.
I love you.

Polos for also dropping everything to come help us. For loving dad through his last moments.

Madrina Mercedes for recognizing that it has nothing to do with us doing something wrong or not believing strongly enough, we all know it's about the passage. Learning, hurting, growing, still loving, still believing and constantly having an open mind. Thank you for talking me through one of the hardest phone calls I have ever made.
Te agradezco todo lo que significas para mí.
I love you.

Maryam for showing me the meaning of friendship, of companionship and for giving me a chance to find the incredible affinity we share. You are the closest friend I have ever encountered and I'm glad I did. Life is easier, happier and simply better because I had the chance to share with you.

Thanks for sleepovers, life talks, teaching me, listening to me, caring for me and being such a supporter in all I do.
I love you, my best friend.

Jose for being a brother. I never had one and I thank you for being there. I know it was hard for all of us regardless of our stumbles, I'm glad we had you. Thank you.
I love you.

Monica, where do I begin?
Do you remember that night you and I had, let's call it a "heated discussion," in the laundry room? It still scares me thinking about it. I can feel my voice vibrating and exhausting my very soul. The four of us were the only ones that have truly, completely seen each other in those low points. I'm sorry if I ever hurt you, I never want to feel such anger nor do I want to target it at you. Throughout the past year you have been very helpful. I thank you for doing everything you did for dad, mom and myself. I'm sorry that I'm a pain in your ass most of the time, and that you are in mine, but I can't ask for a better sister. Even though I say that it would have been cool to have a brother, just for the feeling, I never felt like I needed anyone else outside of you. You have protected me, loved me and supported me through, everything!
I love you until there is no more to give.

Mom—let's breathe.
Thank you.
You have always been the rock in this household. Connecting all of us through our differences. You have played the part of the confidant for the family and you have bent yourself backward and upside down for all of us. Even though you could have fled when you found freedom you stuck it out and helped this family grow. We will never forget that.
You have always been an amazing example for me and you never let me down.
Through the years we have dealt with a small percentage of things when you have taken most of the responsibility.

Obsessions, lack of love, cold hearts, new life, new home, new world, new family, new feelings until the novelty wore off and dad was ready to go.

Thank you for making the decisions you made with him. I thank you for shaping me today.

I thank you for the opportunities you've created. I thank you for loving everyone I love like they are you own children. I thank you for letting me explore and for welcoming my distinctive ways.

I thank you for your strength, stamina, open-mindedness, your faith, your positivity and your love.

I know I fear losing you all the time, but I know I'll always have you and you'll always protect me.

Thank you for being a great friend.

Thank you for being the best mother a son could ask for.

Thank you thank you thank you!

Te quiero muchisisisisisisisisisisimo (de aquí hasta el cielo!!!).

Knighty Man.

For all of the above, the below, the happened, the coming and the now.

For becoming who I miss. I love you the most.

To all of you I thank you.

Lots of Love.

Samuel.

Querido Papa,

I bet you thought you wouldn't make any other chapters in my life. But I'm here to prove otherwise. The past year has been beyond incomprehensible. That in itself is very you.
I'll admit now how I'm fond of such findings. You vault of secrets.

I remember the sun-filled skies. You kept asking me if I was all right. I was. I am.
The air thickened by story telling, by a carved moment, by companionship.
I remember you fevering, laying, and being a stay-at-home dad. I always dreamt that as a possibility and we briefly had it. We watched movies, we talked while mom was out, while the summer sizzled, my world crumbled, changed, we were pals. I'll always take that with me. I know you knew.

My throat shivers as I think of you. My voice weakens when I whisper *I love you.*
I know you know.

You never saw me blossom, everything I showed you was a crippled seed. A mirror image of how you saw yourself.
You know I've known.

It took a crab to devour you entirely for me to understand everything that plants my feet on the ground. Today and forever, my feet will be in the ground.
Like a tree trunk, I'll be your offspring cemented in this world.
The one you adored.
We know you did.

Regardless of how you spoke, you were the most passionate. That's the quality that defied you, but no worries, that will live on in your daughter. The apple from the tree I represent.

Isn't it amusing how these things work? You're more present than you ever were.

It's a hidden complement and I'm sorry that is the truth.

I'm sorry I took you for granted. I'm sorry I wanted to hate you and never could. I'm sorry I questioned your ability to care for me, support me, enjoy me, want me, need me and love me. I'm sorry I built up walls. I'm sorry I protected myself from you. I'm sorry that even though I knew you were trying, I never gave you a fair chance. I'm sorry I never gave you enough time to understand you. I'm sorry that neither twenty years nor our past lives have been enough time to share, agree and love one another. I'm sorry I question what I've given you. I'm sorry I never shared all my words, completely, until I did and your ears were clogged.

I'm sorry it was only last year that started to make sense to me.

I'm sorry.

I'm sorry that six siblings were not enough or what you dreamt of. That it took most of them until it was too late to realize that grudges, jealousy, insecurities, competition and distance were not worth losing someone like you. I'll speak for all of them with all my might, and I can assure you they are all sorry.

I'm sorry your support system from youth screwed you more than one can imagine. I'm sorry they hurt you and abused you. Regardless of what you heard, you deserved the best. Not by mere human right, but by the fact that you were and always will be a tremendous human being. I'm sorry you always achieved what you wanted and heard little from it. I'm sorry that your relationship with them changed what you and I could have had; that our walls own their name.

I'm sorry that you were used for couple counseling. I'm sorry that other people's grief was put upon your shoulders.

You were the best friend a person could have.

You were the best son a parent could ask for.
You were the best father, and I know nothing else.

Why would I have questioned your ability to love unconditionally?
Now I wish I could have something from you.
I miss your hard words the most.
All from love.

I'm sorry a father let you down like I thought you did for me.
I'm sorry a mother would barely hold her baby.
I'm sorry it will take all their lives to assume such position and to realize
that one baby equals their three.
I'm sorry that their depression, their lack of resolving, their spats, their
obsession, their demands, their negligence, and their detachment killed
you slowly through the years.

I'm sorry you were blamed.
Mostly by me for letting it get you down, but I knew nothing and
sympathized none.

I'm sorry I wished that my parents would walk their separate ways. I'm
sorry I put that out there in the universe.
I'm sorry the recycling of events led you to get too comfortable. I'm
sorry it led you to assume the head of the household without any other
position, any other role.
I'm sorry that liberty, customs, the past, the present and the future mixed
in your mind and led you to get tangled, get lost, and get left behind.

I'm sorry you never realized that you were an idol. That *Manuel* was
made for your amusement. And that entire "bad apple" talk was a front,
because sometimes it's scary to understand the love one can feel. And
that love for you will consume her for the rest of her life, just as it has
since you held her and she grabbed your finger with her hand.
She will marry in your name, and like I hope to do, celebrate it by
engraving her offspring.

I'm sorry I never grew interest in you. Without knowing, of course, because I did.
But I never showed it.
I wish I had been the boy you raised to fight the world.
I carry on the fight with words.
You were the one and only friend that understood me completely, regardless, and forever.
I'm sorry that no man, to my knowledge, will ever be you. And I'm sorry I cursed that poor being and sabotaged my luck with love.

I'm sorry.

I miss you.

I miss your voice, stern and unforgettable. I miss your laughter, raspy, consuming, welcoming, endearing, and whistling through the air. Monica and I have it sometimes. I miss your mustache, which I hope to grow at some point. I miss your rough hair, which I think I inherited. I miss your dry hands and your big fingers. I miss you punching me, and the rest of your rough affection. I miss your white tank tops. I miss the smell of your coffee. I miss your love for cheese, bread, and anything good. And for the love of God, may I say, I miss your fantastic cooking (but don't worry, Monica is doing a fine job).
I miss your talent. Fixing, or trying to, everything. Remembering all those languages. I miss you drawing, the one and only time. I miss your musical ability. I miss your barbecues. I miss your bending blue eyes. I miss your smile. I miss your scent. I miss your incessant questioning. I miss your shouting. I miss your loud breathing. I miss your snoring that made any house tremble.

I miss you.

It's funny because now you are just a thought, a distant memory, but with so much strength. It's funny because I sometimes look in the mirror and wish for the grays to take over my hair and I find the things you own on my face over mom because I never felt you within me. I always missed you in your presence. I always questioned my validity.

The hospital fucked my mind.
You thinning did it too.
White halls and empty rooms, of all the people there like you.
But I thank you for choosing it. With it you fortified my life.
I think I share this thought with you:

I've never felt at ease. I loved you so much it detained me from showing you. I've never felt understood, and I talk to myself because I don't think someone else wants to hear it. I've been a loner through the laughter and the friendships. I loved once and knew it was a commitment, not a privilege. I live to make people happy regardless of how much anger I have inside. I still don't understand the huge signs swinging in front of me. But through it all, I'm being proved wrong. I know I can love, I know I'm loved. I know you loved me and I know that everything is possible. Finding people in a sea of millions. Finding souls in a world of danger. Loving through it all. Holding on until there is no more, until the future is inscribed, the signs make sense and the world cries for one name.

I thank you for the obvious.
But mostly I thank you for inspiring me.
I thank you for allowing me.
I thank you for being in my dreams.
As most importantly, for becoming the energy that I pray to, listen to, and aspire to be near of.

Papa, te quiero con toda mi alma y espero que te gusten mis palabras.

Hoy y siempre.
Sammy.

CHAPTER 1

PART III

Stuck
Fighting for a moment

A lifetime of longing created by you

Excited
Fighting for this moment

A lifetime of memories

Know this
My reality
Know that my dreams speak the truth
The days that should have been
I can't let go
In truth because what we have come to miss
Completeness delayed by stubbornness
I feel you on me like a mistake
Bruised like our lack of tact

You and I
What a pair
You know who I am now
From beyond
That I do hope

Stuck
In a dream of humidity
Fingering through
Your presence
Mine only—not sharing anything

But with you

My body aches
In truth with what you said
Breaking down isn't easy
But it's my art
Of decomposing
Taking away your space
From each seam

Each scarlet vowel of I love you

It's true I can't let go
The moment of making you mine

Insinuates the idea of making a whole
With what you left
With who I am

My body aches
My mind is playing
But I resist
The need of lying

I fail

The dreams pile on
Because I need to know you love me back
A simple affair
From months of closing in
Away form years of closing up
Walls
Facades

Tough

Rough
Can't bare the essentials

Not having you near has emphasized the unwanted
A moment of fear
Teeth greeting
Teeth sipping the tears
You showed me strength

Claiming to break

A simple song
A simple kiss
A simple embrace
An enchanted dream

Still afraid to lose what I never had
More afraid about the truth drowning me

Look for you
Knowing I never had what I wanted from you

Closure

Never to have until your face appears along the clouds in my skies

So wait, when will we see him?

The skies have darkened again
I'd love to see your face
A mirage in the clouds
To see the tears run down
Run down such livid no longer vivid face
I miss your laughter
Remembering is hard but I try
I try my best to let it sink in
To oblige to the feelings of loss
Your love never concrete
Now—no longer to see
I fear that this is my destiny
I have the tools
But overcoming seems impossible
Which nothing is
So I believe

Carrying on with darkened skies

"The man will come again.
So wait, I will be ready."

Bounce back and forth

Deliverance
-
Guilt

But I guess there is no easy way to say goodbye

My back shows signs of stress
Hives
Flashbacks

A schoolboy—A good boy
Attentive—Caring

Someone I want to be

Patience disarms me
Waiting to seat on a cloud
Alongside such elegance

Perfect
Each night I can
Putting my hands together
I pray
Every time medicine doesn't take over
Or crying becomes bedtime stories
I pray
Perfect
For almost four months I've closed my eyes
"Padre nuestro, que estas en el cielo…"
Never do I see a man on a cross
Nor that long hair I perceived him as
But you
I pray to you
Even though I always thought of happy things with
Now—the words of the Father the Son and the Holy Spirit
All energy—all space has a new meaning
You
The skies you own
The sun—the moon—the stars
Every time I close my eyes
Asking—searching—pleading
It's you
It's all in one
Perfect comparison to such spirit that flies
Interestingly true how all matter comes from one
Each night I can
I pray
Closing my eyes I see Sebastian

More signs I ask for
Could care less—I want them

Criticize—Scrutinize—Pull apart—Spit on me

I'm not the being I was told to be
I'm weak—relentless & unfulfilled

The lack of *Chaos* in the abundance of who I am

Can I be destroyed?

Unfair chains of life

Why prolong or obliterate
Something continuous?

More to see
Signs—More signs!

I ask for what I know I need

Humor—Contemplate—Knock—Punch me

I'm not going to be who I was told to be
To follow
To search for
Too hollow

To mimic
To love

To succumb to
No more effort

Trying makes you wonder
Wondering borrows from questioning
Therefore questioning keeps you from trying

I ask for signs
I ask to see

Because you leaving took the best of me

Only to wish this is successful
To separate myself from the crowd
To make you proud
Making gold out of misery
Laughing at those days
But no
I rather salivate in my longing
Being the most creative
Honest—Disarming
To bask in the light of constant awareness

Virginia said

Death is contrast

The heroine won't die
But the poet

Why am I here then?
Or am I not seeing correctly?

Are you not the hero?
Or is she?

Were you the visionary?
Most likely-

If not
The citing is off
And my days are accounted for

I hope you don't mind
In my heart and soul
Since I cannot take death back

You are the poet with such lovely prose

Self worth along with scarcity
Not seeing beyond the flesh
Getting stuck past the tint
The mass and contortion of the soul
Wishing but stating that there is not much use
So with quantities and a sense of *pretty* those values never held
Quickly evaporate on giving myself away
Highest bidder—Lowest pay
I give myself away

How can I be honest when I've been lying to myself?

Ave Maria—Purificame
Dios Santo—Llevame a ti
Padre—Contesta mis locuras
Amor—Encuéntrame otra vez

How?
Exactly how could I approach this?
When every sense of truth
Sanity
Joy
And fulfillment is shattered in a moment like this?

An answer too easy to resist
Approval non-existing as it flees

Funny story-
I feel like you're writing through me

Love
The lines across a face
Living showing signs in the unwanted lines of pain

It's nice
I'd say
To have someone to hold and have the feeling be reciprocate
It's fine—To wait

Dislike
These steps
To take to lessen the blow
To walk once again

I fear
Some days
That the memories fade
That I will forget

I fear
Nonstop
About being like this
Liking the dark
Staying inside
Not looking outside
Hibernating the sun
Hiding the hurt

I know
Inside
That is nice to say things

But it's hard to get by

I can't control
The feelings of others
I'm ready to blow

I could
If wanted
Take the bull by the horns
But I know that I won't

I hate
My soul
For being so weak
For clinging to those
Who feed energy
Who care if I fall

To draw the attention
To draw all the eyes
So they look at me
So I am the star

For not loving sooner
Not showing affection
For caring for things
That just come and go

I hate
This life
A year of multiple losses
Of painful regret
I fell off the wagon
Got up again
They took something else

That I can't replace

The longing
The waiting
The knowing the truth
The leaving
The parting
I'm hollow with you

I hate you so much
I can't stand your face
I say this out loud
Not reading my head
Where are you?
I need you
You left me alone
I'm not the only
But I feel my worst

I wish you
I wanted you
I hope that you'd be
Along my
Next to my
Whispering my ear

That love will not leave me
That love will not die
Like you did in moments
One breath at a time

The life does not mean lying here alone

That my future brings more things than before

That you will be inside for the years to come

I will know but not miss you forever—anymore

No more

I love me
I know me
I will never be tough
I need life
I dread it
But not like before
It gave me a gift
I'm forever thankful

I love you
I miss you
I can't stand alone

You keep holding my hands

I hope that you stay

Keeping me company

For the rest of my days

What a run
You were a wonderful man
A great father
Struggling husband
Redeemed yourself by trying
An emotional rollercoaster
Wrapping everyone along the way
What a treat
Your presence
Such a gift of a soul

Dust yourself and try again
You would have never accepted such claim
A wise man you were
But never acknowledged such greatness

You never feared when the push came to shove
You always retracted but not when you could have

A professor until the end
A prophet with nothing more but a pure heart and humor
To share
Pure soul
Hard hitting

We come into the world crying
As everyone celebrates happily
Now you float away with a smile
As the world lays awake crying
Can you tell me…?
Is there a way for you to answer?

Pure Shores

Inpatient to meet you again
For the first time
First kiss
First encounter
Fishily trusting the gut
The water running cold hoping for *Pure Shores*

The visit
A complete commitment
Tangibility
Time constricting
Life convicting
Heart warming toward trusting the love
Vacancy
Inadequacy until then
Patient to meet you again

Fishing thoughts
Scared through to the core
This piece is chocking as it's missing
How can something hollow weigh so much?

Started to think that maybe its just sadness
But you were erased

Nothing to do to resolve that

Now—as bodies take shapes hovering through with the weather
It's more about what's to come
The other bodies to deteriorate
The other voids to make sense but to blur such sense with fear and
reason

It's more about the sentiments of the past
Those taught to be repressed to guilt over
Now—It's about feeling without boundaries

Crying because there's feeling
Smiling because it's thrilling
Fishing thoughts of what to do that now you're gone

White Lilies

Island
Deprived of approval
Overflowing with incentive
They say a man is not an island
You can't function normally
Deviant
Describe such behavior
But I hear a song
It deepens my heart
I can taste the sight of you
A coconut breeze
White Lilies Island
Ruffles
Layers
Distinctive
I don't like how it feels
But boy do I feel you
It's hard not to howl with my eyes
The world is hardly right
So I give you my dry-pouting lips
Along with the benefit of doubt
You drive a green-breezed truck
Weekend vacation
Just you and I
I forgot I had you for myself

I don't need anybody to be
Love is cheap currency
But I'm willing to give the world and beyond for my one and only boy

So I break briefly today
I won't get passed it

I wish I were as oblivious as you
Or as strong
The words you left behind with me
Your one and only boy
Because today anything goes when I hear what you speak

Goddamn
Censoring nothing but air
Puffing from swollen lips
Cursing the days to miss

Essence
Purity
Scent
Dirt between those fingers
The dust across two eyelids
Residue

Strength in cursing
The easiest The softest

Passed on
To live forever
Without realizing
The words narrate it

Taste is bitter
Like the greenest apple

Tongue still likes it
Reasons for pronouncing

Live through me like a stage mother
Forever to feel your efforts inside me

Exhausted
Can't fight anymore
Each passing dream
Hoping to see this was untrue
Willing to feel to hear you
Pondered all the alternatives
Choices
Consequences
If I release the pain through slits—red wine
If I run as fast as it's allowed
Free falling
Physically to match how I'm feeling
To forget you
Simply to allow my sorrow to take me to you
I wish I could go through what you did
To know strength
Learning from perseverance
Stop myself
Nothing is right
Except to be
Content
Fulfilled
Allowing things to come to me
To cry
To shout
To blame
To howl
Yet I'm exhausted
Every night a new dream
But I can't blame you for stalking
I'm thrilled to have you near
Thanks for listening
Contact reached

Funny story —
Could be that I've let the past few days become a blur
Or
That I woke as the morning had died
But life is senseless

Cannot place it in my place

The laughter of the opera
Or the grunts otherwise
The air breezes through—burning my skin
My eyes burn from the freezing water
Or
It could be a reaction from the heat transmitted through tears

How could I find somebody if I don't know where I am?
How could I let someone in if I don't know where I stand?
How could somebody love me if I don't love myself?
How could I have appreciated my father if I underestimate myself?

Not by rules
No plants—no pets—no love interests
I have done well for myself
Convincing myself of my happiness
Reassuring—over achieving the love I share with myself

The mind is clever
Sharing information a file at a time
So I give myself an opportunity
I seek then I shall find
Not judging situations

Giving *them* a second chance
Not me
Only human purity

The fact of the human sin
Even then...I repent

Not to judge—just to be
Self worth along with pity
Knowing—wisely—The answers of the world
Holding too many keys at all times
With my extra—I have one last try

The doors keep opening for seconds at a time
And like a bull—only one go

The past knows
Somehow jinxes
It foreshadows these things

Inside it was clear
On some level
That all of this would disappear

A womb never enunciated
An embrace as thin as that umbilical cord
The one that no one cut
Except the willingness to let you go

Magical
Your last months on earth
Sharing—loving—not pretending
Even though it seems easy to label
Magical
To erase those black marks across your face
Those thorns in your heart—now freed
Nice to see
You left with love
A room of pretenders
A room full of you

The moment happy to teach
A key you became as everyone was moved
But time doesn't heal
It separates learning from living
Numbing such knowledge of caring
Going back to the same old ways

Neglect of the soul

It was clear form the beginning
That nobody would still care about the remaining ones

Crescendo

Youthful angst
Fed through ear plugs
Electrifying neurons
Freeing possibilities of escape

I endure today to achieve
Allowing the past to lay were it can be seen

In case I need to go back
Fulfilling encounter once more
The bed
Soft and sturdy
The winter setting the pace

Downstairs a man and a woman
It's you
It's gotta be
You hold her
Just make her happy
I believe your words
I'll see you later
Worry about her
The lack thereof
I sing along

While you are in our living room
There's a man
It's gotta be you
A tear

Crescendo
I believe in what you do
There's a man
Darker
Younger
Willing to fulfill
It's not you

The man in our living room
How could you?
I miss it
The life we had
Why did we choose this?

Dear old you

I must know where you reside
If not my guilt will devour me
For being the ungrateful child
Even in the end

Worrying about what the future would bring
Me Me Me

The task of making a living
Living green
Waking in the dark
My favorite
How was that a struggle?
Listening to tunes only for my ears
Being the one I want to prove I can be

With your small lips
Stubbornness and charisma
I distort with selfishness
I never said sorry
The ungrateful child

Even now with these tears
I keep you alive for my interest
I hope you flew away
My skin feels tainted
Comforting in the negotiating light

Just want to be like this constantly

That way I feel you
Truly
Without seeing the one that I miss
Troubled
Trying
Hard working you
Loving selfless
Perfect old you

I can't contain myself
Without advice
A hand to grip
My one and only example flees from me

Warm Fuzzies

Wooden box—not just a block
Ability to unlock the power of color
Of what you make it to be and what is not
Ten gifts of words—wealth—flight

All you need is love
All you need is a penny
To make it grow
Stretching what's needed or vice
Faith in questioning
A blessing of sunshine each and every time

The art of hope just like a dove
Simple mundane
A miracle of sorts
Watching the feathers
Grove within the wind
I came across your secrets
Because death tends to need the attention
It's easier to detest it while learning
Seeing signs
Believing the occult
A secret life

Today I sat crying
The open made me content
Someone asked if I was okay
I nodded
They said it must be hard

Getting on with life
Knowing the quality of the deceased
But lack of existence claims no sainthood
The painful demise is what wrecks
Not taking away the lack of tact
The distance among people

Today I sat crying
The flowing air helped contemplate
I simply held to my warm fuzzies

Every waking day
Every sleepless night

The bed is taken care of
The smiles are somewhat there

Forty-seven minutes
To the third month
The moment I know I learned
Life is brief
Memories are horrible keepsakes
Unreliable
Not accurate

Like a sequence of a dream gone awry
Nightmares chocking on too tight

There is a board
Picture frames
There is a hole
Where there used to be a face

No explanation
Not knowing why

Last November was the time to say goodbye

Knowing your words
The mind
What's true—What's right
Reality
Leaving—Sleeping—Not coming back
Death
Appearing like a cloudy cup on the kitchen table
Gin—Scotch—Good ol' Beer
The scarcity of life
Sipping in and out
From the cup to your mouth
From your mouth to your lungs
Can't stop

The cycle it haunts
Tears—Claws into exposing skin
Can't wait for the summer to start
To begin- To run
The heat appears on the horizon
The sun stays up later
The sun becomes company
And the life starts again
Maybe to appear on another face
On the petals on the drive-way

Appearing as a glowing star midday
Can't see

It changed
Such name
No tears in some time

When routine broke down
Depressive child
Smiling now

How can it
Should refuse
Stand up for love
Sit & Think
Remember those memories

Can't feel
The cycle starts again
Guilty for losing you to the ground
Not holding up a candle

Candles wither away
They could have lit up the skies
Fifty-one this time
The year has really flown by

Blue skies
Brown eyes
Remember the comparison?
Remember all the lies?

The past was tainted black
But did you know the future is the same?
It's just not that bad
It's something I now call life

Hands were never held
But minds always alike
Our backs we always hugged
Our love would never die

Did you learn what you did have to?
Or was it all in stride?
Did you feel the pain within me?
Or was I too vacant to provide?

Love has meant loss
Enough to prove the moment
Love has come from you
The one thing you never showed me

Irony doesn't begin to explain

That the one and only
The one to explain
Would be you
It was you who melted me
It was you who let me be

Not in peace or agony
But you left me with enough pain
Enough questioning
To let me find the key

Candles wither away
Just like you are to me
I'm sorry that is lesser—the pain you left me with

Forget you not—but I try
I hope that doesn't kill your insides
Whatever they may be

I know at the celebration of your birth
I was not in attendance

Wanted to
In a way denied myself the fact
A graveyard is the last place to eat some cake
Or sing a song for many more

The last place I want to see

I fear my lack of flowers on your day
May lead to a quick-to-forget person

Me
The only thing I want to see is you

The songs off the yellow brick road
Tearing apart sentiments
From ear to ear
From tears to the unbearable fears

Black and white fingers speeding through a board
Lengthy tongues claiming all I owned

Through a life
Those notes stole away
Through enjoyment
They expanded a vacancy

Now
It's all I own

I cry not because you left me
Not because of regret
Not because of anger
Suffering
Blaming
Escaping
Questioning
Nor love
But because those songs
They fill my vacancy with more air
From a premature childhood
Closet mobbed by skeletons
Secrets
I loved you
I know you loved me too

I don't ever question
I don't ever doubt

But alone in a vacancy tells another story
There's no hope for a future without you
Not because I can't be but because I don't want one
Not without you

When you knocked the table down
Or when you cried until the day said its goodbyes
When I asked the stars why I was not right
Good enough for my father
Or why I felt I must entice such anger
I am who I might be because of such defiance

When you held my hand and warned me not to break
A forehead kiss before the last breath

I long to know certainty

I don't believe in nothing
You are a definite possibility
But life without you
It doesn't make sense

These love songs from the yellow brick road
A one-man band and a silly playing game

I know you're a star
I picked your name from a hat
I know you're not all that far
You're a child in my head

I know I have you until I'm old
To have but not to hold

Can't walk with you
You can't watch me grow anymore

I'll have the best
I promised you that

I know you're a star
With you I've been *Blessed*

A whore
Wish
To blame
Something concrete that one can stone to death

Death
What's the timing for moving on?
For feeling sorry for oneself?

Can't explain
A whore
Wish that could be said

New
A man
Following for years
Happiness it should make
Creating a path
Smile
To hold back such dedication

Hard
A father cannot be replaced
But a lover can

Another entry
Lusting after novelty
Hard as stone
Rubber can't subject to such heat
Melting in the gravel
Melting at one's feet

Seeing is believing
With vacancy You don't exist

Grey suit
Hanging in a closet
Hope it fits
Attempting to regain nostalgia
Lost it
The moment I smiled without remembering yours

The moment I heard *Goodbye*
I sobbed like the child I used to be

Living *Forever*
With the sands of time
Can't grasp—hold—nor divide
The feeling of empty and the feeling of life

Realized a dream
Wish you could see
Share it with me
Dancing in a stadium
Crying tears of skin
Chilling through the bones
Standing all alone
Not knowing where to look at

Grey
My favorite
Blending all the colours
Holding heavy tears

Hope it fits
Smell like a man

Never to become
Never to see the day
You died before I had a chance to
Now I'll have the dramatic stay

Wearing your grey suit
I stroll away

Miss beads
Coffee feeding the vents
Taking over the morning light
Miss your breath as I went to class
You would be racing away
A kiss on my cheek
I miss
The feeling of stubble across my chin
The feeling of a man who would protect
With love
Struggling the morning mass
Miss beads

Air is non-existing when I miss you
To remind me of my breathing shortcomings
I'm sure
After all —
They all came from you
But I do —
Miss
Heavy breaths
Each sound you made with that mouth
The lack or air
You made it work
I miss
Slurping your food
Bread—Cheese—Wine
You'd die happy
Hoping you did
I miss
The snores that like an airplane

End up soothing the night
The house trembling when you lay down
I miss
Discomfort
The kitchen tv screaming in Italian
Raffaella Carra or Lucianno
Who also left
Ti amo papa
Non sto bene perche ti amo. Molto.
And I miss—Molto

Politics
I miss my adversary
My opposite
White tank tops and the wheezing of your throat
The best laugh runs in this family
But you—demure—I miss
The last time I heard it
It turned into sobbing
Each and every time
I blame the chemo
Radiation
Sometimes the world

I miss you completely
All your faults and never-ending stories
I do
Each hug we ever shared
The time you punched my arm
Pretending to box
Your passion for DeNiro
Seeing you enjoy your great music
Each Sunday morning
Asking your blessings every night
Kissing your face along the way

Miss beads
The coffee taking over the world
At work—At home
Your trademark

Constant Reminder

I write today with tears
Blurring every line
Thinning the very essence of my format

This confidant is my only salvation
Yes
I don't allow
Accept
Won't deny
I'm as closed as my book on the shelf
Untouched
Well kept

Unfortunately
I've taken from you
Instead of visualizing the steps
Enjoying the virtue that you were

Today is your day
It has and always will be
The chill of the tree branches swinging melody
Like mint opening every pore
Welcoming the light of sunshine

I'm dry
The tears stopped falling
But that's not what I mean
I will be a prune lacking the taste
The juice of life

I will until I allow otherwise

A dedication unread—misheard
Will be my constant reminder

The sun was covered
My favorite the week ends or starts this Sunday

Pretty Little Birds
Life has never been so sweet
I bet dreams are made of this
Easy to disagree
As the days remind me and I miss

A beat—A reason—A song for this empty season

The leaves have fallen
The birds surround me
There is no song
Since you I love
To love
To see again
A chance
My dreams—sweet indeed
Have been coming true
How unfair for you
Unfair to know
You won't be coming back

At night—The day—A cruel reality

The love I have for you
Immense in proportions
Leaves me vacant like a vase
Filled with beautiful flowers
I see my surroundings
I breathe the air around me
But if you ask me
I can't remember

Not the air—The smell—Your face

Only regret with disbelief
Contradictory
I'm a prince
Surrounded by empty kingdoms
By pretty little birds
I have dreamt this
It would not have happened if it were not for you
For the empty love I'm living with
The past a fantasy
Playing back in my mind like a movie
The future I cannot see

The horizon line ends eventually
All I have is all I need
A beautiful today
With eyes for pretty little birds

The light no longer keeps me captivated
Nor in disguise
My feelings have found me
They won't let me stride
I cry as the sun shines
I lay bare as the moon lights the skies
My heart with its desires
My dream, fears and lack of gravity

My father passing hasn't let me live
I see simple things I enjoy the idea of such dream
Being aware and completely giving in
But I don't and guidance I lack
I hope and pray at night—in the morning light
That such idea changes and the matter becomes the fact
Emptiness captivates me
Disguise becomes my being

I wish that the light had kept its stance
So I would be able to be productive
Work to live and live to breathe so at night I could sleep
Now—I don't sit still
Creating excuses for my lack of living
A book full of information
A lifetime worth of love
A future so uncertain
Hovers
Killing every part of me

The future is something that I hate
I look forward to it
I hate it!
I can't imagine myself anymore in any situation
As a lack in the space around will only make me wonder
Make me wonder what ifs and buts
Can't control—so I'll want to stop it all
Inside there is turmoil
Melting the soil
The ground beneath
I creep through the days
Smelling the air looking for a familiar scent
A face I can hardly remember
The music plays
Reminding of the ideas of memory
A dream
A movie
No longer playing
No longer in existence
The reality of the carnal
The physical world and its absent love
I carry on
Alone within my body
Aching through my wondering
I can't explain the pain inside
The suction of life through my pores
Through each tear I try no to cry
I can't complain
Life has been kind
Bu all I want to do is run
Away from memories

The ideas of such dream
I used to have a father
Now I have nothing
Nothing but a picture
Fades
Nothing but a memory
A dream
Nothing but abstract
My favorite
I start to disagree
I can't believe the feeling of empty
Almost created a friend for life
Time was everything but enough
Everything but a smile
Drawn on my vacant soul
I salute you father
Hoping you are truly part of me
Making me a man
Strength to overcome
Not to break
Not to get lost
I love
I cherish
I hope
Optimistically
Childishly
Maturely
But the walls keep melting away
Like the white dove flying toward you
Through the layers
Taking away a feather at a time
Melting its shell
Too long of a flight
Too long of a fight
With myself

With your words
A memory of so long ago
I can't fathom
You gone
So in my head
A business trip so long
That day-by-day becomes a truth
I used to have a father
I could have been a lover
Because it feels as vacant as if I were
A dream so fragile
Wishing you still were

Simple Words

Wearing all of your socks
Looking through your old phone
Holding your stuffed pup
A way to be with you
The days that once were
With lack of you already
Follow me
Frames of time frozen
Haunting
Simple words between you and I

Droppings

Slightly depressing to know that not even a dream
Of birds singing only to me
Becoming a reality will make me feel at all happy
All I think about is the worst

In abundance
The bird droppings or evil in any form
That's the cold
The best of seasons
Will leave me frozen in a bed with fluids squeezed from my body

I don't retain such information
Since my father passed away
I become the one and only man
Strong enough to evade any type of disease or incumbency

My father killed by lack of breath
In a bed for longer than a while
What's to be expected?
From the weakness within me

I hope not to break
Yet irony is all that's left

There's no input
I won't break like he said
But here's a shadow
Of years of hiding

From fears
From crying

I look back
Alone in the dark
Flew the doors open
Shedding a tint at a time
But the time ahead will be
A struggle in itself

I've shown the power inside
Willingness to try
Passion to help
Power to make it
But today I won't drive
Because my name is too weak
My intentions too sweet
A man I'll become
There's no second guessing

About that now—ever

If you were to close your eyes
Setting the trees on fire
Destroying while you bowed out of your character
There would be a heart that would skip a beat forever
The idea of your body hardening like a freshly baked cookie sets a timer
A timer on the days ahead
So I won't let the mind wonder
About that now—not never

A job A task
Just money For a life
I lack persistence
Balance though I seek
I sit all but tranquil
In a home that falls apart
In a room thickened by dust
In a heart bruised because
There's nothing to fill it
A job To work
Fulfilling the dreams I may have
Dreams of achievement
Goals to follow and calendars to fill
Checklists Boxes Checkmarks
Paper sufficient to free souls
Green lucky enough to feed mouths
Make dreams erase the pain
There's nothing like this
A job A step
Closer to those clouds
Flying high on happiness
Though there's a hand
A set of eyes following my star
An image The dreams
You spoke to me
I held you tight
There's no guarantee

There's a picture of the day
When I went away to find some clarity
The start of something I could call my own
I sat trying to figure out if it was important enough
The picture on my wall
Of a person I wish I could be
Rich
Passionate
Strong
Admirable
An example
An honor
For a woman that has given her life for a family
To a rock that has helped me through the smug
To a roof of what I used to call a home
To you
A father that never saw what I could do

This picture on my wall
Represents who I can be
A person detached from all else
Willing to be happy for a moment
Wishing Hoping
The picture of the day your death began

Honor
But I can barely keep my work up
I sit today
Sick as a dog
Subconsciously
Sabotaging what I have left
Not going to work
Thinking of what to do with my life

Uncontrollable Cough

My maturity is not real
The hairs along my forearm
The sense of thickness
I drop my priority for sensitivity
Simple cough remind me of my frailness
The one I share with you

A year ago, where were we?
I was dealing with another loss
Ignoring you completely
After you held the door open for future and I
Lasting sixteen months
You
Twenty years
I made a mistake
So I wonder if today
Before
I told you how much I would miss you
That I love you uncontrollably

Instead I cough and wonder

The enablers in your life
All of this fault came to me in my dream last night

The way it was not right but still okay
To smoke your sad smile off your face
The way it was wrong but letting you drown
Your liver and disappointment with your liquid

The breath you painted
Was cruel and empty
Like the cadaver you became
Sad but true
Pale and thin
Stretched within your own skin

I wish I didn't feel it
So strongly inside
Letting my dreams speak for my mouth

The rooms of vice
Separation of levels of foolishness
A doorman straight in his stance
Staring at mine
A doorman gay in his persuasion
Holding my hand as I walk inside
A party in the darkness
The rooms I have frequented
The places made for youth
To kill them while they're plump
Full of cash to dance away while sweating the excess

I saw my home
Falling apart in the ruins of the night life

I ran through doorframes and anxiety
I opened one last door to find you panting

A white room
Smoked through to the corners
A hospital bed with you laying
Smoking a fag
Like the one you had for a son

I kissed the doorman on the way out
As I scratched the life out of my sister with my words
I was bile
I was right
All along
I can safely say that

My mother I cursed
In a dream so obscure
That I saw you how you were
Once you left the earth

An outcast I have been all my life for standing my ground
Being too different with my standards
Leaving a husband
Keeping my lips closed
Citing time after time that we can stop ourselves

Your parents were on it
Once life killed their organs
I saw this all of my life
And still I'm the one that isn't right

Well
Today I can say
I told you so
And curse my sister and mother
But I won't
For losing a father
There's no point

Instead
I weep
Knowing I miss you
The dreams become me

I see you
I warn you
I pity you
I despise you
I need you
I want you

I'm with you
I love you

My life
I always thought I'd lose it first
You beat me to it
Always competitive

I've realized mine has just started
I've just accomplished to graduate from high school and lose the first love
of my life
What will happen next? I hope is the greatness I dream of
But in those dreams
You take strong pose
In those dreams you are part of the whole
What will happen now?
My book is to be published
Will you get to own a copy?
I dedicated it to you
If I graduate from college
Who will be to my right or to my left?
It seems my mother by herself
I wanted to get married and have you crying there
When I adopt a child and when my life starts making sense

I've wasted my life hoping for something to come
For our relationship to flourish
But now that it began
I won't see it growing strong with time

You have haunted my entire life
With empty words
Silly ideals
Trying hard

Now you will haunt my future
Strong love
With comprehension
For the rest of my life

My head echoes

My eyes were glossy from the tears
I didn't notice I was crying
The pain has done well with camouflage
My dad's sickness has kept the house up
And the constant coughs makes the walls tremble
I want to be able to escape
I've tried
To dinners and friends
The movies I've seen
But now I sleep less
My head succumbed to the worst of headaches

I can't think through this pain
Now I've found that in my family my hopes live on
Slain by the mockery of trivial love
A hand to prematurely hold mine
Whispering sweet words

My head is overcoming
I hear my thoughts but my sight is blurry
I must sleep to overcharge
But now that I've found my light
In my family I must reside
To help this home build itself back up

But now That I've found the light
I reside where I reside
Why does my head echo with ideas of a life?

Submerge myself in loss
As if my chest reversed itself
Trying to get out of my body through my lips
The tears so thick drying my veins
The blood no longer pumping but clogged
Standby
I can do that
Anytime
Every time I think of your last breath

Drowning in memories of could have-been
My skin tight and tense
Much like yours
Pale and tinted yellow
As if rusted
As if rubber
Never living
Again or before
The signs of souls fleeing
Leaving their shells behind
Laying coldly on a crowded bed
Painfully seeking liberty

Shocked
I remember over again
About such frailty
It stops my body's functioning as if the thought would disappear
My eyes swell
A body is missing
The substance

Submerge
I drown

Today
I see your smile

Remember
I can't
But wonder if you do
If you know
If you feel
See my pain
I can't explain
I wonder if you can

Can you see me today?
The way I long to say I love you?

I'm stuck on this feeling
But I don't see you
Or feel
Don't think of you
But of what could have been
The way you left
Nothing else

It's weird
I don't talk to you
But to thick air
I use your pictures to help me remember
I can't on my own

I look into the sky
A gray coat
Covering who I am
Who I'll become

Do you know how I feel?
Are you ever close to me?
I wish I could sense your presence
Your scent

Can you see me today?
I can't

Three months cut dry
A life
So sudden
Taken back
Wishing memory could
So that the world would spin around
Faster
Three months since last
The beginning of a lump
Driving down a lonely road
Leading to nothing but work
Sockets to feel
Feelings to show
Showing the love
Not loving enough

Three months not even
Cutting the ties
Last time I drove
The start of a demise

Hugging
It helps to soothe the pain
Tugging
Inside out & crying out loud

The loss of a loved one
We ask ourselves
Where is the power of The One?
Are the eyes that trace every step
Veering to the ground
As we keep turning to the left?

Can you question the power of such God?
That lets the heart bleed?
A necessity
Quite
Unnecessary

Touch is inhumane
That is why I crave so
To love in such a way
That the skin belongs to us
Not I
Not he
But ours
Completely

I stumble upon a pebble
White in its substance
Dark in its appearance

Picking it up I find
It's led me to a grave
The place is desolate
From years of knowing it was there
Not realizing it would be his resting place

There is no sign
No way to show appreciation
But the moving sky
With clouds in one direction

They speed as if they tempted
Moving grief for a gratifying reason
I knew it once before
The sentiments engraved in stone

One that is not here
Along with a body
A soul
So vacant
It flew over my head

Hugging
Tugging
Kissing
Holding
Wishing
Praying
They all do nothing

An entity is questioned
An alternative is chased
But
The light is shines right over my head
The stars they sparkle just as I look their way

A hand it sets on my forehead just as I go to bed
And if fireworks mean anything at all
Then life has much more to offer

Death
Hard to write about
Harder to let out my mouth
I believe in it wholly
Knowing is not the end
But a better beginning
That higher we do embrace
A powerful light
It happens to the best of us
But we only believe through sight
When a body gets cold
With hands not grabbing back
Our spirits fail to soar
Becoming stale as our smiles
It's hard to believe
Believe that the love still holds a light
Close to being alive

Though death does not equal not living
We don't have the science of life
When we begin—When we end
And all the reasons why
If the universe occults the place where we land
Once our veins are clogged and worms eat our tact
Then there is nothing to fear

But when death comes for my father
It's harder to believe

I left the bed the week of a departure
Once love fled
Through my veins toward the exits

Sleeping on a couch
Bending by the tears
Kept on rusting with them

Days became empty slots of luck
Nights reminded me of him
So I stopped
Tried to keep control
I failed
On the couch I slept each night

Answers are eloquent if not found
Love is not real if not felt
If not seen
If not called upon
To caress
To hug
To admire
I seek
Never have found

In the future I see
In the past I've lingered

Today I can't imagine
How she sleeps on her bed
I can't really tell her
But I don't think I could make it

I wish not hope
Blues
Remember when they haunted me?
I know they will
The presence of those eyes
The lack of stability in a lifetime
I searched through seas so clear
Darkened by pain & fear
Never found a match
Wishing—Not Hoping—To watch them attract me
To know they control me
Consol me
Those eyes had such passion
Such a life
Why couldn't I see the distractions in your body?
I feel ashamed
Never the same
Someone to blame
The constant struggles between us
Something to think about
I do
Still
About how you left
Swiftly but truly
I can still feel you
Within me
A kiss on my forehead
A handshake so firm
Yet subtle
Gentle
Fading

No longer
If I don't break
It will be for you
If I drown in my blues
It will mean more than you'll ever know

I wish not hope

Hug you tight

Big eyes
Small mouth
Big love
Quick words

You left me stained
Now feel true pain
Never will I search again
Watching over me

Never will I feel the same
I can deal with that
Never will I See your face
Touch your hand
Hugh you tight
Say hellos or goodbyes
I can't fathom that
The idea kills me
Slowly
Every waking day

I don't want to live like that

Big love
Not close to enough
Lucky to have you

Just showing how I long to hold you tight

Gasping for reality
A picture
Blue eyes
Nothing's the same

Cold hands
Only remember
Bruised skin
Can only remember
A truck
Parking memories inside
A closet
Not going inside
My dreams are a never-ending movie
But while waking
The terrible nightmare begins

Gasping for air
Pinching my skin to stop this feeling
But pain only elongates what you meant to me

Start a new
Missing you slowly
Looking back
That's all I seem to do
A picture in my hands
Eyes blue with terror
I need to run to gain my sanity
To inhale the life out of every being
I will
Try

Subconsciously
A goal
Emptiness

Blue seas
Empty love
Not enough air
Just looking for love
Lost it as you began to elevate

Fireworks within shinning stars
Snow covered rooftops
They lack persistence

Wet crying eyes
Don't have uniqueness

Today like any other
A day of remembrance
Today like any other
Life flows through

The trees—the roads—the people I see
Nothing matters—how you did to me
Nothing holds meaning—faith wants to flee

I'll look at the stars tonight
Hope you guide my aching heart

Dancing snow-clouds

Midst
Sweat
Tears of regret

Relied on the idea
But long for answers

Love
Trust
Honesty
The world is not enough

If the constant wondering can't succumb
The idea won't let those thoughts go

Today your scent walks through the air
Today the idea of a dream keeps falling from the sky to my hands
I pray
You stay
In my heart for the rest of my life
That I can bed the idea
And not long for anything

Gay ol' time
Bells are ringing
Choirs are singing
But there is no truth in meaning
No real lyric to be singing

Emptiness and sorrow
Limbs missing not in war
Miss kissing my father's hand
Mind racing through gifts & joy
No hidden play
Through tears & aching hearts
Can't find my father's hand

Smiles keep mocking
Chocking the meaning of birth
Not stopping to think
Starting to feel reality sink in

Terror filling lungs
With powder not from guns
Not a bomb
But a lump
No bread crumbs to feed
No more mouths that breathe
Just a body buried deep

Songs glisten
Words are missing
The meaning of love
The meaning of a shining star

This time you'll be faint
This time we roam again

I'm sorry
Because I fear
That life is pointless
That love isn't near
I carry
Day to day
A burden
Guilt
Worry
To myself
Not sharing my grief
I sit and weep
I'm mad
Sorry for myself
I apologize
For being so selfish
Letting pain take over me
For missing you like I do
I see the signs
The learning begins
But I can't stop
Thinking ahead
Fearing a future
Regretting the past
Loving you slowly
Seeing your smile
I'm sorry
Because you were in pain
That I wasn't paying attention
Too busy worrying
About what to do with myself

That I cannot seem to help
I'm just taking space
Filling up air
With empty words
And being alone

I'm sorry I see you at night
I'm sorry I cry on my own
I'm sorry I'm doubting God's ways
I'm sorry I'm not in my home
I'm sorry for fearing
I'm sorry I cling
I'm sorry I'm useless
I'm sorry I'll never see you again

Golden Boy
Too heavy to carry
So much baggage
So much crying
Life has not misled
Or misplaced us together
But for reasons known
A life for the greater
Puzzle
Perfect proportions
Unified
Connecting the dots
Our lives will never be the same
Since the trail has been for you
Since the beginning of our time
We began as a foursome
Now we could end as one
Even plentiful
Additions as we become nomads of the land
I couldn't be myself without you
I wouldn't care the same without you
The fact that you hurt me deeply
It's the reason I still stand
The idea to demonstrate to you
Your love
Today I'm empty without you
Healing slowly but surely
Keeping my distance since I feel I got a piece of you
Letting other enjoy
Lucky I've been
Knowing so soon why

The reason for our relationship
The turmoil—the whispered tears
I love you the most
Because I know it's been heard for you
You've tried the hardest
In positions like today we fear
That life will bleed through us
The pains of the entire world
Either you - mom or myself
I cherish your words of trust
Honesty and disgust all the same
Life has shown us the best of paradise
Awareness
Now I can sleep better than before
Knowing my attempts to find love

Questioning the world
All lead back to an obstacle so thick
So thick I can't think
Think about you leaving
But I will let you do your thing
Knowing is hoping
Life is anything but a game
We don't get to play
But live
Extent of what we give
Receive
Through your lips I have heard enough
But I wish I could hear more

I wish I could hear you say enough
Say the entire world
I don't know anymore
But I want you safe and sound
Exempt from all this trivial mess

The tears still fall on tightly held hands
Through your lips I have heard love
I guess I won't hear you say anything more

Golden Boy
You've been to me
To us
A connection to a future
To our past
And why we are like we are
You've been the glue to our distinct home
You connected us with the skies
Given us more to try
To see
To feel in certainty

I miss you as I fall
I cry as you lay
I don't know what to say
But thanks to the Golden Boy

My chest is drenched with tears
Absurd how I still can breathe
But I do
Photographic memory
Instant
You
Blank
Us
Instant
Steam
Black
You
Instant
Love
White
A tender smile
Midst
Instant
Instant
Instant
Light
You
Blank
No more
Instinctive endurance
A simple pamphlet
Blue in its wholesomeness
In big thick font
On top—reads your name
A program of your death
I open the paper

Instant
Scent
Blank
You
Instant
Grief
A priest
Dark
A casket
You
Blur
Glare
Light
You
Closed
A chapter so absurd
The soul it flees
The skies welcoming
Energy received
A peaceful remembrance
Yet I can't let go
Because I simply don't know
Give me a sign you're not in pain
Give me a sign you're doing okay
Memory
Blank.

Casket full of joy and full of life
That is what I want to see
I never dreamt this day would come
I can't put you away yet
I want to know that you are sleeping
Tired but content
I want to know that you will wake
See the day just like yesterday
Planning this will kill us all
But I am the man now
I must be strong
I know your place I will never fill
I don't cook like you
I am not as astute
I will try hard
Now I have help from the second boy in line
He will do better
But I will carry the name
I know my sister probably will too
You know you are her idol
That will never change
So between us all we will care for mom
She won't be alone I promise you that

Today you lay in the hospital bed
I'm thinking about the day that you are ready
I will try all with ease
I will be the man of my dreams
The man you always wanted me to be

Just like you

CHAPTER 2

PART II

Howl
The sound of SOS
Mouth dried by the water
The one melting the insides

Taste wasn't an option
Lost it once the laser hit skin
It never helped
Ironic?

Thick
Losing grip
Bones took over
Shapeless
No more of a rock
No less of a man
But lacking the strength once possessed

Mind lost
Reality wasn't the same
Not crazy
Just not the same

Missing it now
Even the alteration
Had a piece of meaning
At all times

Cry
Like a wolf toward the moon
Not full

Not in the near future

Wasted time worrying about feelings
About loss
About a future not to have
Lost time
Regret
Pain
Throat swells
Not able to swallow pain
Lingering on a voice
Not strong enough
So it comes out on paper

Memories erased from a lifetime lived
No smiles
No laughter
Thinking of those
Kills softly
Prefer to think of the ones
Fresh
The lingering pain
It stays with those behind
On earth
Remembering

Hands wrinkled by liquid help
Cold by the demons inside
Attacked by all sides
Couldn't help it from happening
Apologies
Feelings sorry
For such weakness
The power of the mind
Letting the world win
Again

Memories
Shaking feet from side to side
At the sound and glance of a caveman
It hurts
That laughter

Like pins and needles
Walking barefoot on dry ice

Walking alone along a tombstoned grass

Memories
Struggling to walk
Getting help to be mundane
Letting feces lead the way
I was your maid
I don't mind
But as memories fade
That's all that can be found
In the back of a head
So scared and down

Rest such case

Physical world

In an instant everything drowned
One last breath
Shifting pieces changing dreams
A reality to think
It chokes the life out of the rest
Lucky ones to carry on
Painfully creating an uncertain future

Impatiently sit crying to myself
Expecting more of life
Expecting more to dream
My face it drowns
You—Can't live without

In an instant I'm myself no more
In your eyes I saw the wonders of the world

Pink rays of love
Pink rays transmitting to his body
One power Eight bodies
One circle of trust
One moment not to forget
He cried

You've been the glue
To all of our lives
The Golden Child
To bring us to today
Love
Strength
Stamina
FORCE
BELIEF

CURED.

(We tried.
We did.
Inside
You fled.)

Sky
It always knows
It sets the mood
Clouds
Darkened by sorrow
Heavy with tears
It didn't rain
I love it when it does
This time my hand
Groping what's left

His hand fragile but stern
His eyes closed but knowing
I spoke

Remember
No matter what happens
We'll make it through
There is a wedding to attend
A friend waiting at home
My work to be published
Words of love
Fear of loss
My life
Dedicated to you
Always
Remember

Strong
You say I'm the strongest
Irony
I guess we are not as different as we thought we were

You are the strongest man I've ever met
A purpose A gift An example to follow

I know I am not the man of the house
I will never be
But I am happy to accomplish
All the things you had in mind
Not to bring myself down
Or to forget who I am
But to follow the footsteps of the man of my life

You
Connotations don't begin to explain
The strength within you has had no limits
Not beginning today
You will remain
Through our eyes
As the reason

Torn
I promise I won't break
Don't worry about my body
I won't be condensed
I learned from our mistakes
Neither a substance nor a dream
Will affect the life left to live

I cringe at the sounds of the crickets
The song of summer you might not hear again
In body
Your spirit flies away
Slowly but surely

Strong
I learned from
You shared so with us
I'm cut in half by your departure
Losing a sense of why I live
But then again
We don't give up so easily
I begin to see the light
You shine on me
As you say goodbye

You fear me breaking
But I won't disappoint
I cried at your sight
But together we are
The man and the boy
That never gave up

Strength comes from knowing
Knowing led by searching
Looking for the reasons
Thinking through the seasons
Being okay with awareness

A closed book no longer
You open with such brilliance
So much knowledge
With vigilance

So much strength
How could I not follow

Frail
Never before
Forever a delicate flower
Hard to believe in decay
Floating across the ground like a cotton ball
Scratching the tiles
Leaving imprints behind

Heavy
Empty
Hollow
Heavy

Sorrow
Anger
Fear
Regret of the days that once laid

Angel
No wings to fly
But you did
Across the gray skies
Through the clouds
Toward the stars
Shine

Hard to believe in emptiness
Hollow
A shell
Flown
Never to land again

Or does it happen

Believing has become a task
An effort
A complicated reality

Strolling along
Holding a metal
Walker
Stalker
Dreams
Faces
Distortion of love
Lust after your star

Floating like a pair of doves
Sliding through the thick air
During injections
While perspiring dust
Those feet would wiggle
Never touching the cold floor

A song
A whistle
Through teeth not able—now lacking
Remember those days?
Now the sound from speakers
Making your heart pound

A caveman with anguish
Not feeling humanity
A walkway so lonely
And harsh stereotyping
A billboard so large—you could hardly miss it
The tune of amusement with toes unresisting

Happy is good to have
Knowing laughter was to be had
A memory to talk about over dinner
Yet the head of the table is empty
The one making the moment is lacking his righteous gratitude

Paper thin
Hardly recognize the man in front of me
Skin is paper thin
His eyes are ajar amid his weakness
They wonder around as if my face—my name were vast

His hand is shaky
There's pressure mounting even though there is no movement

I miss you already
Won't recognize the fact that I'm in history
Dissed by statistics
Falling behind
It took us years to get here
For you to get sick
For us to be near
The irony
Now
As close as we can get
You're slipping away

It's hard to recognize
That it was I in error
But I need to clarify that I have no blames on my table

I wish we last longer
I wish you stay my buddy
I pray to you: Don't die
Because I started to miss you already

Psychology
Anatomy
Not caring what it means
In my dreams you still exist
Memories
Ideas
I never had you close
But I always wanted to feel you

It's funny that the way eyes chose me
Is the way you looked at me
Cold and distant
Crystallized blues

The idea of two men
Together as one
The sweetest of sights
The more you realize
The more it sinks in
The love in between them
Will never be clean
But pure in their hearts
To love each other like this

I care about you
I miss you the most
Because I never got to know you
The way I should have before

Signs
Symbols
When is one able to know the difference?
In regards to reality
I pray
That is all I do
Believe
Because without it I'm nothing

You lay
Weak
Telling stories and asking questions under the influence
High
Weak

Your life is a story to be told
A partner with unconditional love
She sits impatiently
She prays emphatically

Mom had been there for the entire month
Hasn't gone home
Sleeps—eats—showers next to you
In that room
She waits

You turn to her
With her hands groping yours

I guess now you can finish your book

You can't do this to her
You can't leave her alone
After all she has done for you
Who will care for her?
I will! I will finish the job
Why would you have me to then let me go?
We just started bonding
I miss you when you're gone
I can't believe you would leave me
Leave us
The strongest family I know
Will that change?
I don't know
Just tell me you won't go
I won't let you go!!!
You can't die yet
You're far too young

You can't die yet
Then my love will go
Floating in the plain
Where will you go?
I need to know where to look
When the hands of the angels take me too

I sit patiently
Hoping you are safe
Knowing is hard because I can't see
But love is strong and belief makes me tough
I will now let you go
I never loved you enough

Empty bedroom with no bed
Absurd to limits
Absurd in my head
The matter of the fact is
I've pictured this before

Can't deny the fact
That the towel could be dropped

Think back and remember
The days I used to dream
For you to go away
That way our family
Complete and effervescent
Could float across the plain
In air bubbles so thick
Nobody in this world
Would ever hurt again

I wished you walked away
My parents to end
But now I'm so afraid
That you might not stay here
Now there's an empty room
The room that lacks a bed
Then you might not be near
That this could mean my end

What am I supposed to do if I don't want to talk about you anymore?
It's hard when all there is in my life is your status
The fact that my schedule changed because of it
The lack of presence in the house too
The visits from the most random individuals
The reason why my sister cries herself to sleep
The incentive of the dog's depression
I sit
Wondering if life will give something else to talk about
Another chance at love
At life
How am I supposed to deal with this if I don't want to?
If I don't want to go where you are
Or talk to mum—anymore—I can't
Everyday I try to place my presence so you know I care
So everyone knows
But by laws of the world or my lack thereof
I feel I'm better behind the scenes
Specially because I can't deal—anymore
I dread seeing you
I'm sorry
I can't stand talking to her
It depresses me
I avoid my sister at all costs
I don't want to care

I cried all the way home last night—again
Alone
Because if I show more
It doesn't make sense—it doesn't help the matter

So I become the hating child
The selfish prick
Only worried about finances and not being able to chip in
Emotionally I'm drenched
I know all of you need me
But I can't deal

I'm sorry

In the past two weeks I have gone back to ground zero
Feeling you fade
Crying only inside
Avoiding your face
Avoiding my mother's voice
Avoiding the people that need me at home
Hating every minute of my days

I cried already
I made peace with you dying
I was fine
In two weeks I have lost my efforts
Dealing only with avoidance

I don't want to stop by the hospital anymore
I don't like it
I wish I could not think about you every second of my days

When people ask how I am
My answer is your name

I can't fathom this
I can't
I had already
But now that I am back
I refuse to think about it

Through these emotions
I lack strength
Wasting my time
Not enjoying what's left—if anything—of you

Of the feeling alive

Crying is back
Dealing with you is my life again
Today
I think about it thoroughly
Knowing you are a priority

Sleeping is appealing
Not feeling
Also
But I think of you
Instead
Loving you
From far away

I sit on my ass everyday wasting everyone's time
I sit only hoping to be released
Taken care of and pleased
Mentally—Physically
I sit on my ass everyday doing nothing

I'm not worth the money I get paid
I am not enough of a son for nobody
A brother—Not enough

Daily I ask for support
Never giving back
I don't do anything but wonder about my life
Playing with people's minds
Hoping to get a thrill
Mentally—For my eyes

I can't take being alive
But I'm stuck
Until I die

After you're gone
After we're all mad

Daily I see my life about fooling with ideas
But doing nothing about them
Knowing truths but shelving them
Stocking them into a room of no attendance

If I am not worth loving
Then I should make peace with that

If I can't change my ways
I will be the same asshole as today

Sitting on my ass again
I can't help but feel sorry for myself

Textbook

Says who?
Whoever wrote this doesn't know me—like you
The idea that everyone is equal is beyond me
Our reality denies that—yet not in all that's abstract

Yes—I defy

Roller coasters—laughing until crying are two separate emotions
Stale to vicious words—I don't try emotions
Behavior dependency—I'm not refusing anyone's help

Textbook? No me

The pills that took away best friends—acquaintances & strangers—even
my father!
And I have his small mouth—his dimpled chin & a full head of hair
Even his stubbornness
But I've spent a lifetime to differentiate
If I can't take the list away—Then I'm at least avoiding the next

Dirty hands of love

It's like a Phoenix burning inside of me
That passion transcending toward a new being
Building itself up and trying again
Dusting oneself off and bursting into flames
A fire lit from years of tranquility
A light so bright for guidance

There is the idea of Gaston
Such power Such masculinity
I cherish that in the pieces I lack
Would not consider holding a mold
The picture of strength and grasp
The idea it brightens my eyes

Ashby was left behind
Ideas of a wholesome union
Divorce took the name away
Can't plan the future with any old ways
Ashby completing one being
Separation took away my offspring

Like a Phoenix bursting into raw energy
The ground gravitates toward destruction
Such power and tranquility
Allowed not by earth's grievance
Creating a new will be an untamed foal
Finding a boy in the dirty hands of love

Perforate

Changes one night can bring
A moment through the midst
A struggle
A stumble
Sudden stop
No longer able to carry on

A light is darkened by moves
Body out of sync unwilling to resist
Air lacking strength to pull up
Tear down defenses
How one should
Controlling the place where we come from

I guess I avoided the entire subject
Not wanting to prepare myself for the undoing
Now I must decide to overcome
I understand now why those decisions are so strong

The names of my future seed
Sebastiano
Giancarlo
Antonio
One will perforate the lack in my life
Growing stronger as time can mend

A hand in my hands
A tear of the bed
His emotions out in the open
Importance one moment can bring

I'm still your son
I know you love me
I love you back
More than ever
Since you lay on a hospital bed

Though the feeling took over me before
As if I felt

The past months have been bliss
I feel that finally we are both in a place where we can enjoy each other
Laugh—Cry & share

I know I am not the son you asked for
You don't need to explain
But I tried my best—in my way—to make you proud
More than other sons have

I know I am not the man you wanted your son to be
I know that my lack of masculinity has & always will be a disappointment
Not blaming you
I know you are still trying hard to overcome that and love me for me
Which you do
But that will always be there
Not the son you wanted

I'm trying so hard to take your place
Not just in case
But to alleviate your load
And become the man of the house
Yet I feel you don't want that

Mistrusting my abilities

I want you to be proud
With everything I do
By taking care of the house
Won't do it for you but for necessity

I criticized my first love
And sacrificed my life because of approval
As I keep trying to find yours

I am now done
Hoping for the best
I know you love your son
But sometimes it feels like you do less and less

Today
Brand new numbers
An age not old enough
By some months
A digit
A quantity of siblings
Never near
Aspire

Skin boils
Insides infected
Like a body once caressed
Hugged
Held
Perplexed
With ideals of a life

Good versus Evil
Beautiful intentions taking the lead
Inner smiles taking the price
Aura white as snow on a Sunday night
Moral
Immoral
Perfection
Willing to learn

The world is not enough
Stern
Large
Comfortable
Enough

To want to walk it
Through & through

Age is just a number like the days that lay ahead
Hope is just a bird with bruised wings
Love is too complex to want to define it

Yet the past is still the past
With nothing to look forward

If a body vanishes
Where does its energy float?

In times like this is hard to comprehend
I allow you to flow through me
In moments like this—fearful we become
I won't allow the pain to set words upon my world
Yes—loss is immense when the love is so strong
But the world moves with your direction
In your path only trust can reign
So we allow happiness to show through the pain
Things happen for a reason
The reason in the best of interest
It would never be horrible
It will never be wrong
So with movement of emotions we find ourselves again
Trying to comprehend the facts of the matter
All we need to know is the path is a clean slate
Happy is never bad
Loss won't take away what we already have

In times like this I wish I were a rock
To put away my feelings
To put away the shock
Love had ruled my life—now—what will happen to that love?

Bipolar

Always too eclectic for my own good
But now it's different
I cry
Loss is hard to deal with
I smile
I know God's intentions and I see them through
There is no problem in fear
A normal atrocity
There is no problem with me
Within abnormality

Being so open is a great quality
But now it's the same
I keep fearing
Loss is very mundane
I keep trying
I don't know where it leads—so I can't believe
Not trusting will be a demise
A dream that is horrid
I just can't believe
I try—I just can't

The sense of you leaving is making me shiver
But I must think of others and not of my pain
The signs of you withering are making no sense
Yet the world still goes around—I must be there to accept it

I want to love you
Crying to show you

I want to be stronger
To show that I can

Now I sit
I drive
I sleep
I eat
I live
Crying
Smiling
Sad
Happy
It's making me crazy and I don't know what is right

Weakness
The moment of one sweat
Muscles aching
The usual mess
My head in despair
No longer tasks
No longer work
No pressure to finish
But of an abrupt end
Mucus
Lengthy in meaning
If it was strong enough to kill
Not knowing until he was brittle
Mistake
Then—will it end my stance?
So quick—not painless

This home is scarce
So much love we had
So little time for the retained
The glue of strength has left the household
The empty space has made her fragile

He has her
She has us
Two to four

There's always been an understanding
For each other we do anything
So strong love inside us
After new territories tried hard to make us crumble

Four to five
A new brother
A new son
Another mouth to feed
Another hand to hold

Two pairs one solo
We have our fallouts
But always understanding

Four to five to four
Two pairs no holes

If I'm made to be her soul-mate
I'm willing to forget

As the ground starts shaking
Shifting paths
Moving a solemn stance
Life begins

Without your kiss
Life will move about
Finding other lips
Holding onto doubt
Slightly
Shifting with the tide
The ground
With the skies

Memory is nothing but a state of mind
Numbing reality
The very essence of which we once were

As the love starts growing
Distance does too
Grasping for what's known
Life is a stint

Without your hands
The world still turns
Holding other palms
Finding other truths
Surely
Getting by
With drowned eyes
Day to night

Memory is nothing but a mirage
Swelling dreams to live
Living the very essence of who we are

Today
Feeling you fade I cripple myself
I write fate—scratch & start again
I shouldn't let my mind wonder
Guilt stamped on all my thoughts
You are plugged in as if the life
The life in you had flown away

Looking at you I cripple myself
I feel as though a void had been sitting
Begging to complain
My whole life I have been searching
Highs and lows to confide
A face—a body—a soul
Into that void

I still do
Search
I still lay
Alone

But I long to find a lover
Half a man
At least half a man of who you are

I stop to think
Wonder in the subdued lights
My shadow against the glass
The floor filled with dust
Where once a person stayed
I realize

With heavy tears across my face
Indeed my fate could be
Spend the time ahead like times before
Looking to fill the void he left behind
No more room to grow

There is yet another question in my head
Possibilities of your passing away are making my head go
If you no longer provide for your lack of being
Who will be my father?
If a father figure settles in my life
Will the one who signs my paychecks become the figure I will no longer
have?

If your eyes no longer sparkle
Knowing you are not really looking at me
Watching from afar
The images that come my way will make my head go
Knowing the signs & symbols do rule my world
No longer like you do

There was a child within me
For reasons of joy—of dependence
Now that ruler fades
A child of grievance
Loneliness & fear
I already cry when I think of you
What will I do without?
I miss what I don't already have

There is yet another thing to analyze
Scrutiny of the future makes my head go
If you no longer hold my candle
How long will I have to wait?

I wonder now
With all of this movement
Remember our lives? I don't—I didn't have one
But changes we chose
I wonder if
If the future holds something for me
Now that we might chose movement again
Leaving this empty place we call home—Mine
I wonder then
With bodies taking up space
But yours lacking
Will the family leave us again?

Now we'll embark on a journey three to the set
Additions are always welcome—but the originals stay in my head
Movement might take what's mine—hypocrite—selfish—Changes I fear
With those—the American Dream also flees—slipping away as you are

I wonder now
If I will lose my head on the course of this trance

It means the world to me

Midnight bells ring in my head
I have never liked time
But I have no excuse for my panic attacks

I have let the weight of my clothes fall on the world
Now the rest of the world lets its clothes fall on me

I thought I'd be easier
But things keep piling up
Now I am stressed
Trying to make a buck
For me
For my dreams
Plus my family
Plus what we mean

It means the world to me

Now I have a horrible headache
Keeping from my rest
Names and places come to mind
I thought about selling what the rest of them want

My body is fragile
But I'm willing
To make a buck
For my reasons I'll do anything

I have let the weight of my pain fall on the world

Now
The world has dropped a ball of work
Can I handle it all?

If it means the world to me —

Love from last try

Hallways demure me not
They try to intimidate me
They try hard but they don't
I strut away
I don't know if it's the irony of the hospital walls
Or the hospital bed
The smell
A tumor taking space
Inside my father
Inside his lung making him choke on his breaths
Maybe the structure lacking in my life
I don't know if it's such irony
But my heart is still full
From the start
With what's left from my last try
A smile paints on my face
Oblivious to the sins of the world
I walk without a destination
Hoping life rules regret
That love is mine again

Spirit fragile
Walking toward an entrance of deceiving qualities
Many possibilities
I strut reluctantly
The sliding doors open breaking my heart

A deadly robe steps out
Swiftly

Black in the absolute with a book to match
The white line across his neck was minimal for reasons of hope in the
drowning of the rest
His crucifix lazy on his hand
After squeezing the faith out of it

His head bowed toward his feet
Walking swiftly
Matching mine reluctantly

The doors closed behind me
I kept walking without directions
The thought of my father sunk my throat to my stomach
& my stomach peaked through my nose
The two switching motions on & off
He would be laying once I saw him
He would be squeezed once I got to hug him

The presence of the black robe made my walk complete hell
Walking as if lonely—by myself

I sped my steps but I slowed when I thought

The idea of my father
Was not a sight to see or a place to be
If the father was there for mine
& for lack of the word became the one to have
Then why would I want to walk inside
Toward a destination of faith & hating every minute of it

I took one big breath staring at the wooden door
It taunted the ideas in my head
I took a big gulp of air
Held my head up high amid the tears
Walked in the room
& such sight should appear

Question of respect

Letters are not subtle but informal
Why claim care over words?
You hire You pay
Yet when falling you don't care

Falling ill can be such a burden
Not on self but on a family
On those who depend
Mouths to feed Bodies to clothe

Falling behind should be an emotional trial
Not professional satire
Money transcends the pain and agony
Money is currency in an awful exchange

Falling ill is a question of fate
Daddy worked himself to crumbs
In needles through his pain
Being human is a question of intent
When words have left your mouth
There are others empty still

Being human is a question of intent
Daddy deserves more
A bit more of my respect

CHAPTER 3

PART I

Postman

Faint
Stronger
Absence
The power of
Lacking
Stalking
Speaking a tongue
To someone that is listening
To the one who stands above
The world threw you a curve
The tree let you fall hard
Missing embrace
Reassurance
Faint presence
Strong will
Absent character
The power of guilt
Today you spoke no more
Creating a child that would no longer live to love

Postman II

Obscure
Delighted
Dark led
Still lacking
Still stalking
But in a world of wealth
Your soul still strapped against the wall
Beneath the starlight
The world is in you
Through your eyes I can see
The worries of sin
Lay gently behind them
The world put you down
So did your mother
But the hurt that you call onto another
Is simply a note that's made to consider
So do yourself a favor
& post it
Get rid of the note
Once something's in writing
It haunts you no more

All my life thought you were a pervert
One time even thinking that "friend" from the liquor store was your whore
Your other woman
In childhood all you did was get fucked up
Outside of crying begging for the world to stop
Cussing the hands to grasp
A wooden table tight
But not a soft baby
Blaming others that slapped with wooden paddles
That's all I saw
Saturdays were a show
Sleeping in to save energy
The show after hours missing
Through the years I'm shocked
You didn't hit the bucket sooner
You never loved yourself
Nicotine was a closer friend than kids or a wife
But I learned
Quickly & suddenly
After getting over child scars
Mental blocks & hating who you were
Understand substance abuse & no self-awareness turned you early
Too quickly
Unaccredited artist
Drawing better than anyone I've met
Controlling your tongues for each occasion
Building a mini empire from leftovers
All you needed was awareness
A softer touch
Disregarding those who hurt you
You were never a pervert
Though you smelled & acted like one
All you ever were was a child in a man suit waiting to arrive

Blue eye fetish
Started
By your face

Know that we can't let go
You hated me for being so free
You never allowed yourself to be

A man
A lover
Curious
Willing
All of the above
In a mixture
In a being

Blue-eyed monster
You hunt my mind
As I sleep
I see those pools
Empty of life
Heavy in meaning

I missed you the moment I met you
I never held you
Never to think I would

Walk the line
My father forgot to hold me
He was too distracted by his mold
The footballs rolled past my stance
The distance between us started to grow

My father forgot to tuck me in at night
I was too preoccupied by doing so with him
By age seven I had my own child
To take care of
My worries began

There has been a void
Which took years to comprehend
To admit
Trying to mend in any way possible
To fulfill this untamed love

I search
I do
The faces of my father
Those I bed
I opt to fuck for being un-kept
The softness of a manly touch
An ideal
A figure not to look up to
But to control
This is my way to prevent
My heart from breaking into pieces

But not a controlled balance
Fatherly love I have lacked
Now my partners walk the line

Rolling ball

We didn't get to play ball before
I didn't like it
The fact that you wanted me to
Still hurts me

No matter what—I'm your son
Regardless

Talking would have done wonders
Thank God for his strength
I'm no longer a closed book
& I'm able to share my life
Unless it's with you

Sometimes I fear losing you
But I feel like I've never had you
Our relationship has grown
But we still need to pull through
The lack of you in the past
Has made me who I am today
I don't ever want to blame you
But the distance between us remains

You are my one and only—You will never fade
All we need to worry about are the days that lay ahead
We get to play ball now—I like to see you happy
The fact that you never tried again is the reason why we're actively
smiling

I think of you as my soul mate
Maybe too stubborn to learn that with lives we shift
That no longer we belonged to one another
That you were no longer my lover

Never holding each other too tight
Repulsed by family ties
It's hard to capture an idea without an accomplice
So this with me will die

I long to have you near
After years of distance
Trying to dive into memories
To rescue any clues that may help me heal
So your face doesn't disappear
Within the tears the concept nor the years

I think of you as my piece to the puzzle
You brought me to prominence
To a bright future
Filled with freedom & A Dream
You lend me a hand to get another start
By you leaving
I strive to be your better half
Strive to be your only one

We shift
From a son
To a father
No longer lovers
But a future in the skies

If by loving you I punched you
If by caring you made me cry
We'll have a future in the skies

The day was amazing
Completely filled
One of those late year-
Winter ready-
Holiday craving-
Goddamn—I can feel it!

In any other world

I can feel you completely

The day was nostalgic
A Friday—usually exciting
Usually eager—Usually

It was damp—it was light
It was dark—it was getting cold
It was

You—Me—Them—Us—Then—Again—As once before
I can't take it - I can feel it!

Say goodbye to the world we thought you lived in

You never left
Violins never played
It was an awful dream
With my future in a box on my steps

Is The Glass Half Full in any other world?

Every morning—weekend & summers & days off
I'd wake prior to you

Quite an achievement

Dawn—still owning legitimate darkness
But cleansed

Walking door through door
Seeping the air conditioning—the heat—cold air again

I would notice you two sleeping
The bed with leftover covers along the foot
I'd make a bed & roll into a family

The frozen ceramic—the chilled thick material hugging my skin

I've always been lonely
Do you recognize that as a gene?

The bedroom—plenty of space
What a fun architect
Kind of shitty but fun
The bathroom—a weary memory
But I remember the cool bathtub

I used to play with my toys for hours
Prune-y became I

But I can surely remember that light switch
The one on the wall toward that bathroom
The very look of it
The way the plastic broken made the point of protection impossible
The cables hovering over the nothingness

The screws
The very look of it
Abused

That will never fade

The moment your rapid fist created a crunch in my ear
The pieces flying
I hovered above you
Above nothingness for years

I never asked you

"What is your name?
Wanna be friends?"

XX

Incantation
Strings through harps & guitars

Gypsies—Royalty

Sweaty summertime
Three generations

Sitting—Listening—Complete company

What a load—Music library

The night was wonderful
But it did end with an ache

XIX

Four kids when you only bred two

What a father—How deep the love

A broken child
A basement pad
Straightening the nuts
Screwing me back to my reality

He wasn't it
But time spent would have been with you

Regardless you pressured your questions
My happiness is the ultimate

You love me & I know it

XVIII

Turkey dinner
Christmas exchange of favors
You did for me

Migrating south like a broken-winged bird
You loved me

I put my hand out to marry
Kids stuff really

You reeled me in
Opening doors
Making plans
Loving me

We never left the house alive

XVII

A new home
New floor plan
New us
Painted walls
Newborn pups
Freshly cut grass
A new world

Air to breathe
Playfully outing calendar
Growing pains
No more hateful kids
No more screaming *retard*
Closer commute
Amplified room
A new world
A better one

Thank you for bringing me here
Day to day—I thank you for something else

XVI

Iron extensions
Pumping residue
Sweaty summertime
Well into the winter

Hair shimmering with golden rays
Face smoothly retaining vitality
Rosy cheeks
Orange aura

A sudden apprehension
Quick lived dissolution
Compromise
Complete attention

Rave—Clarity—Trying

Love was fleeing
Stopped
You never let it

The cover of a future paper booklet
Youth became you entirely
Willingly

XV

Faux-consolation

Two thousand & two
When faux-dykes freed me
My liberation was still inconsolable
While walls advised me of Big Brother
As my passion took over
Problems of isolation
Fearing the hand that fed me
Now without that support
I can't see past it
Losing the blaming game is bitter
But not having a being to be the complaisant is an unwanted thrill

XIV

Mission accomplished

Knock on a bedroom door
Wake up! It's late!

A quick bite to eat
Half dressed running out the door

Green truck
Comfortable—like you
Stern
Reliable but stuffy
Cup holder drenched in coffee
The other filled with coins

Silent ride

The cars kept moving
The radio ran its course
Or my personal request that I brought between my arms

A bookstore
Some music
Light reading
More coffee
Ya? Are you ready?
Green truck
Chain-smoking
Cup holders—still stuffy

Silence
Rare words
Distant stares
We share the love of art
Soothing the heart
Together

Funny—then—how aware of my talent
Knowing we were awkward
Yet willing to try
Knowing we had to do this
For our sake
It helped
Since these are my rare one on one memories of it
Mission accomplished

XIII

Sissy little me
A two by four
Apartment living
Once freed from desolation
We were freed into damnation
Reversing roles of a giver
I shaved precisely my preteen stubble
She hid in loving the boy in trouble
The booze never missing
The gates never closed
A woman with reasons
Reasons she never chose
Nor did him—nor did I
But we wanted it
Badly
To run away from a hellish town
The beds to argue & shout
Miming heavy words
The bathroom walls made of liquid lies
I heard your heart beating through those insults
Worries of whores & boundaries
Of control or sissy little me
I heard
I lived it like the nymphs upstairs
As they washed the lust off their bodies
You played
Two thousand
Millennia that made it its task to finish us
We began to grow stronger

Against each other
Against the tide
You had me—a weekend child
I loved your time but never an easy ride
Never a willing try

XII

Wednesday

I call it hump-day for a reason
More personal than weekly woes
It was a sign—escape to rely
On the idea of homosexual
Of who I was growing to protect
The night darkened by filth
With a gentle breeze stinking of angel dust
The air suffocating pores
Drying them to a pulp
The rocking chair swirled
The monitor—twenty five the most
Gyrated with opaque colors
Each more—one moment
Enjoyed by frisking getting caught
Still didn't distract me form you lurking around
Maybe one night
The one time the good shit was on
You stood to get an idea from your maternity desk
That night as I watched soft core
You stood in my doorway

XI

Mammary in a predicament
Scrotum in a twist
The moment you take the neck from underneath
The head starts to spin

Erratically

One night to enjoy
Friday
A country club of sorts
Kids spinning
Skating parking lots

Night fell hard
The moment it caressed
The idea of the kids
Wanting to go out to play

The time had come to get
The mother from the workplace

The presence it had vanished
The like could not be found

The home was still not valid
The calls never returned
The night it seemed had fallen
Too hard on those easily derailed

The night kept going
The drinks kept pouring
They kept on calling
But the calls never returned

The father planning
To blame one being
About his loss
One night to kill

The shouting matches
Began to rumble
The walls inside
Begin to crumble

He blamed the faint
For wanting fun
Not realizing
He drove himself

She felt betrayed
Worried still
She screamed at him
With all her will

He rose his arm
Palm wide open
She looked inside
He almost did it

He cried instead
Dismissed her birth
Slammed the door

She wept outside looking at wood

The gates they opened
The mom had come
A friend drove her
After the night kept going without a car

She entered the house
Examining the ghosts
Hugging & kissing
Not liking the worrisome

It's all okay
The moment passed
The father broken
Began to cry

Behind closed doors
The night had ended
But still drunk
The mind won't let him

It's fair to see the shock it brought
Losing the glue
To all he had

X

Tyrant
Walking through downtown
Freely
Like a prize for being
Being silent
Mother treated us one day
The evening devoured the sunlight
As we made our way back
Surprised
A window was missing from our car
Looking in there were remains all over the seat
The car seemed different
Seemed tainted
They stole nothing but our sense of security
We drove crying
Perplexed by the idea of the chosen
All side by side
But it was our lucky car
The tears began to subside
As the fear was mounting
In the house awaited the real test
As we explained
Our fears of him hating us
Or minimizing mother with his blatant stare
That's the way it was
The respect was owed to him
Excitingly—his response understanding
Worried for us—exclaiming to stop crying
I know these customs leave much to be desired

But by the way things were
You were not a tyrant
As I saw you to be

IX

Nine
Late teen by measures

An adult in a kid's life

Old little man
Just who we chose to live as

A summer—A surprise
To be the kid of the house
To feel freed from tearing up negatively

Patting someone's back
A giant mouse—A black rat
Companions elevated
With a dream of happy endings
In a world I'd come to know
To understand

It was a sacrifice
Choosing whether to give away
The much-wanted approval of love
You know how it goes
The feeling that caring is a prize
Keeping it away from routine
Waiting for a good deed or a perfect moment to confess

You did
Overflow

Both loving parents
The castle
Fireworks
Truly magical

I remember the reason
Becoming close to your son
A method of buying
By putting out with love

I don't recall verbalizing
But your trying made me
Fulfill who I have been
Years passed but I found
My father in 1996

VIII

Metal tasting morning
The body's way to entertain—teach—scare
Family's arrival—hiding with a swollen tongue

The plague of multiplied beings
Spreading quickly
Tearing the white steps
Opening the door to find you
Lonely
That day you taught me *chess*

VII

The years leave residue
Dusty memories
In 1994 we changed
Our outlook of the mundane
Traveling abroad
While the kids were distracted by the circle of life

Cell bars as high as our inhibitions
We played together by ourselves

Locked in an office looking for reasons
A familiar voice or face
With a piece of a name
Determined with the web in your hand

I never knew who you were
Didn't understand why tears fell
With objects meant to break
Why we feared the world
More strongly the person that you were

Now—with abnormal reasons I think
That I feel what you always felt
I know I made it my job
To become the one you regret

Opposite views to the days ahead
The voice of strength not to create
Hope that was a useless distraction

Because whether closure of death
I fear you missed my love
I fear it daily

Nothing could compare to the leftover guilt & abundant
Loss running through my freezing veins
Heard of such sacrifice
Coming from the one

Now I know you own a piece of who I am

Mirror image of a train wreck to come
Dry coughs for two weeks
& counting
Maybe from leftover smoke
Today
Fourteen have passed
But you are as present as you ever were
Inside
The world I fear
Don't feel
I only miss

VI

Woke up at dawn to get a glass of water
Walked to the kitchen—a reminder of the previous night
The breakfast table diagonal to the floor
Its convex legs concaved toward the wall
Bits & pieces making a nasty pattern on the floor
Eyes ajar but not stepping on bolts or screws

A hand at fault for the damage
Human force under the influence
With the help of the light from the window & the sound of sparkling
water
Eyes become accustomed
The mind starts to remember

What a night

After being gone for hours that day
Worrying the three bodies in the house left
Fears of his body's remains
Scared at the sight of the father limping through the doorway

It wasn't the best
Took a sip putting the glass in the sink
Spilling the water down the drain

Three feet tall
Rubbing the tears with a sleeve
Looking at that table
Wondering where the rage came from

Not fond of the *ruler*
Scared of what's to come

I walked slowly into bed
Covering up just wondering

Where will we eat breakfast today?

V

Constructing
Preparing
A hole—Wet 'n Wild
The neighborhood kids wished
What you made reality

Every weekend before lunch
Submerging
During the Sunday heat we melted
The foursome
Fifteen—twenty feet at most
We made the best of it

Every weekend we melted with you

The neighborhood dad wished
They were as attentive as you

A distant-present father

IV

Taking flimsy envelope
Readjusting hope

You had a friend of a friend who knew the guy
White beard—big gut & all

Two kids with too big grins

Every year
Snow did not fall
But a father never lacked

When the tree filled lit
We knew you kept your promise

Knowing a friend of a friend who knew the guy was an edge
Making you a pretty cool dad

III

Salt in the air
The coast
Waiting for revival
Sat together we saw the girls bathe
Walking toward the water
It was like the moment had stopped
Worried—Scarred—Happy—Content
To be with you
The moment like a frozen picture
It still stands
Knowing we stood behind it

II

Horses—Midst—Family
Lying or not—you loved it
Ridding for the first time
Remember bits & pieces
But I can still remember your embrace
Hefty glasses & tough beard
The low temperature—no match to how you've loved me
Sweet memories filled with pleasure
Remembering my guardian angel

I

Opened balcony
Death could make my men unavailable—as they are alive
Or me—emotionally

Shy of two my first memory of incense
First recollection of flowers—insects—tears upon cement
You held me as my old man died
My favorite—first grandfather

The balcony was away from the sorrow
Or maybe because your lungs needed some feeling of filling
But you held me
Protected
You became better with babies when I was grown
But then—I remember
The first memory of you

Wooden mattress
Liquid dreams
Winter sight
A scream knowing what was going to be

Lovely words

La mia mama non desidera provare

Non-voglio
Pensare

The moment a soul is welcomed
A baby refuses to comprehend
No voice
Too brand new

The pain it desires
The moment of truth

But
If a Lioness doesn't come forth
The baby knows it too

WOMB OF DARKNESS
SHINNING IN THE SKY OF AMALTHEA
TWINS
APOLLO
ARTEMIS

DRINKING THROUGH THE VEINS OF A FATHER

BEING ONE TO COMPLETE
BEING THE FLAVOR OF LIFE

FEMALE TO MALE

NEGATIVE TO POSITIVE

INTROVERTED TO EXTROVERTED

YIN OF YANG

THROUGH THE VESSELS WE ARE

YOU'RE THE GOAT SWIMMING IN MY SKY

IN LOVING MEMORY OF MY
FATHER

SEBASTIANO LORA

**JAN. 18TH, 1957—NOV. 20TH,
2007**

Rufus87@AOL.com
www.Theglasshalffull.net